HONOURING

TO
SUCCESS

Apostle Courtney McLean

Dear Reader,

It is important that as we walk with God we do the things that will help to make our journey successful. One of the most overlooked areas is that of honouring. As you read this book I pray your spirit will be quickened and you will see the need to give honour to the men and women of God working in the vineyard of the Lord.

This book is designed to be a guide to spiritual growth and development for both pastors and members, on our journey to spiritual success. The testimonies are included to showcase that faith in God does not go unrewarded.

Friend, there are several other testimonies I could share with you. If you are desirous of hearing more great testimonies of God's goodness to his people who seek to honour Him, please contact Worship and Faith International Fellowship and we will send you a CD recording.

Sincerely,

Rev. Courtney McLean

Table of Contents

Topic	Page
1. ENDORSEMENT	i
2. ACKNOWLEDGEMENTS	iv
3. DEDICATION	vi
4. INTRODUCTION	vii
5. **Chapter 1** Honouring God	1
6. **Chapter 2** Honouring Through Giving	19
7. **Chapter 3** Honouring The Five-fold Ministry	33
8. **Chapter 4** Honour Your Paster	57
9. **Chapter 5** Honouring All Ministers of the Gospel	87
10. **Chapter 6** Honour Through Vigilance: Beware of Wolves	101
11. **Chapter 7** A Culture of Honour	109
12. Declarative Prayer	118

ENDORSEMENT

Bishop Courtney McLean is a man of great value to the Kingdom of God. I would say, God has given him the most powerful healing and deliverance ministry I have seen in the Caribbean region.

Notwithstanding that, he seems to possess the anointing of an Apostle on his life. He specializes in dealing with church health and growth.

I know his writing will turn your life and ministry around. He writes candidly from a wealth of biblical knowledge and practical experiences. As I read through the pages of this book, I could feel a very strong anointing on this work.

In the Body of Christ we need more men like Bishop McLean, who will become standard bearers for the Kingdom. He not only preaches on honouring God's servants, but he practices this as well. There is no preacher I know that has given more, financially to his own as well as other ministries, than Bishop Courtney.

Receive wisdom from the Pastor of one of Jamaica's fastest growing churches. Let him take you to the gateway of success …

Prophet Michael Carter
Pastor and Founder The Dominion Center
Kingston, Jamaica.

Pastor McLean's book is a roadmap to honour God with our hearts and not only with our lips. It teaches us that in honouring persons God placed in our lives as spiritual authority, we also honour God, and that obedience to God's Word qualifies us for His reward. With clear and practical examples of his life, and more importantly with the Word, Pastor Mclean teaches why honouring those in authority is essential to finding God's favour and blessing.

The book challenges readers to think about how important it is for persons to treat others with respect regardless of their position in society.

Sharon Stephenson
Director of Consumer Credit
Unicomer Jamaica Limited (Trading as Courts)

ACKNOWLEDGEMENTS

Igive God thanks for all I've experienced especially during my years of labouring as an itinerant minister in the Kingdom. I thank him for allowing me to write this book in His honour. The negative experiences have also aided my ability to speak on this subject, therefore I can truly say, *"And we know that all things work together for good to them that love God, to them who are the called according to his purpose."*

I give God thanks for my loving wife Nadine who supported and encouraged me along the way. I must acknowledge:

- Novea Henry for her support and encouragement.
- Shawn and Delcita Franklyn who honoured my family by going beyond the call of duty in assisting my wife and I, thus giving me time to complete this book and
- a true and faithful son in the faith, Dale Sewell for doing such a wonderful job in designing the cover of this book.

I salute the ministers of Worship and Faith International Fellowship (WAFIF),

- o Reverends: Elise Atkinson, Thelma Samuels and Howard Reynolds.
- o Ministers: Oneil Facey and Angela Headley.

Thank you for undergirding and helping me fulfill the mandate of God.

To my hard working secretary Tracy, and of course the members of Worship and Faith International Fellowship (WAFIF), thank you for your support.

DEDICATION

I dedicate this book to all the pastors who have laboured and those who continue to labour in the vineyard without honour or appreciation.

INTRODUCTION

There are many Christians who never came into their full potential, never walked in the overflow and never achieved success. Friend, there are principles laid out in the word of God and if these principles are followed, success will be yours! One such sacred principle that was practiced by the great men and women of old is the principle of giving honour!!!

If success has been eluding you, one reason for this may be your failure to honour God and the people he has brought into your life. The Bible says *"for them that honour me, I will honour and they that despise me shall be lightly esteemed."* **1 Samuel 2:30b** (KJV).

There are many who do not realize that by honouring those who labour in the *word*, they are honouring God. Over the years of doing itinerant ministry, I have observed some of the unnecessary strains and pressures which are faced by God's ministering servants. The reason for this stems mainly from lack of support as well as ignorance among those they serve.

The truth is many Christians have not been taught the importance of honouring those who have been placed over them as their spiritual parents and leaders of the flock. Many ministers toil daily without any form of support and recompense. This leaves them feeling abused, unappreciated and disheartened.

Many churches have yet to maximize their true potential as the members have failed to honour those who God has placed over them. This failure to honour God also results in their growth and prosperity being stagnant.

My prayer is that as you read this book, the spirit of God will stir your heart and cause you to see the importance of honouring God.

1

Honouring GOD

*Wherefore the LORD God of Israel saith, "indeed that thy house, and the house of thy father, should walk before me forever: but now the LORD saith, Be it far from me; for them that honour me I will honour, and they that despise me shall be lightly esteemed." **1 Samuel 2:30.***

The Strong's Exhaustive Concordance defines Honour as *"value, money paid, greatness and esteem"*. It has its origin in a Greek word meaning "valuable." In fact, the Greek word for "without honour" literally means "no value," and lightly esteemed means "small." In the New Testament, the main Greek word translated "honour" means "to praise or to revere."

Giving honour is an act of reverence and respect towards a worthy person. God is worthy to receive the highest honour because He is above all - His supremacy is unquestionable. Giving true honour to God requires the following:

- **Surrendering Our Lives Totally to Him**

In honouring God it is important that we give Him first place in everything. Total surrendering will ensure that our lives give praise and worship to Him in all things. Remember what He said to Israel in **Isaiah 29:13:**

> Wherefore the Lord said, Forasmuch as this people draw near me with their mouth and with their lips do they honour me, but have removed their heart far from me, and their fear toward me is taught by the precept of men.

We should ensure that our honour to God is not limited to lip service but that it is accompanied by actions flowing from the heart. What can you do for God with your life that will clearly and emphatically state that you are honouring him?

- **Allowing His Word to Take the Highest Place in Your Life**

God's word should be valued and esteemed above everything. We honour God through obedience to His word as the word of God is a light unto our feet and a light unto our path (**Psalm 119:105**). Matthew 6:33 states, *"Seek he first the kingdom of God and His righteousness and all these things shall be added unto you."* I have never had the experience of being fired. Wherever I have worked, if the job required me to do something that contradicted the word of God, I would state my conviction on the matter. If I was ever forced to comply, I would simply resign.

I remember working for this company that wanted me to practice unethical business principles to increase their income. To put it plainly, they wanted me to steal! The truth is, I needed the job at that time, but the word of God is clear on that. *"Thou shalt not steal"* **(Exodus 20:15).** I discussed the matter with my employer, who said that it was his way of doing business. I later wrote my letter of resignation and left.

One way to honour God above all else is to be obedient to His word and not compromise. As a result of honouring Him, He will release several blessings in our lives. We must put God's word first and resist the temptation to compromise when under pressure and He will honour us.

- **Honouring (Valuing/Esteeming) All Men**

To whom do you think honour belongs? **1 Peter 2:17** states *"Honour all [men]. Love the brotherhood. Fear God. Honour the king."* and

Hebrews 13:2 said *"Be not forgetful to entertain strangers: for thereby some have entertained angels unawares."* You may have missed your blessing or visitation because you overlooked someone who did not have a title (Pastor, Evangelist, Dr etc). The Bible says that we should condescend to men of low estate! **(Romans 12:16)**. We should not just reserve honour for those who are in authority or leadership positions, but everyone. So, remember honour/value/esteem all men!

- ## The Giving of Our Resources

Proverbs 3:9 says *"Honour the Lord with your capital and sufficiency [from righteous labours and with the firstfruits of all your income"* (Amp.) This means we should give to God first. Let us say you have a guest visiting for dinner, would it be honourable to eat first and then entertain your guest with the leftovers? In a similar way it would not be proper or honourable to take care of yourself first and then God's business with the "leftovers".

Consider the account of Cain and Able as depicted in the narrative in **Genesis 4:1-7 (KJV):**

¹And Adam knew Eve his wife; and she conceived, and bare Cain, and said, I have gotten a man from the LORD.²And she again bare his brother Abel. And Abel was a keeper of sheep, but Cain was a tiller of the ground.³And in process of time it came to pass, that Cain <u>brought</u> of the fruit of the ground an offering unto the LORD.⁴And Abel, he also brought of the <u>firstlings</u> of his flock and of the fat thereof. And the LORD had respect unto Abel and to his offering:⁵But unto Cain and to his offering he had not respect. And Cain was very wroth, and his countenance fell.⁶And the LORD said unto Cain, Why art thou wroth? and why is thy countenance fallen?⁷If thou doest well, shalt thou not be accepted? and if thou doest not well, sin lieth at the door. And unto thee shall be his desire, and thou shalt rule over him.

In this account, it's not just what we give but how we give. Cain merely **brought** something from the ground but Abel, honouring, valuing and esteeming God, gave God of the **firstlings**. He gave the first and as such God had respect for Abel's offering but not Cain's. Always put God first and He will honour you.

When we examine the Old Testament, we learn that people, who went for counseling would always seek to acquire a gift for the man of God with whom they meet as depicted in the first encounter between Saul and Samuel in **1Samuel 9: 6-8:**

> *And he said unto him, Behold now, there is in this city a man of God, and he is an honourable man; all that he saith cometh surely to pass: now let us go thither; peradventure he can shew us our way that we should go. Then said Saul to his servant, But, behold, if we go, what shall we bring the man? For the bread is spent in our vessels, and there is not a present to bring to the man of God: what have we? And the servant answered Saul again, and said, Behold, I have here at hand the fourth part of a shekel of silver: that will I give to the man of God, to tell us our way.* **(1 Samuel 9:6-8 (KJV).**

Friends, few people today follow this principle. Do you see how far we have strayed?

- **Giving Honour To Those Who Labour Among You**

Giving honour is an act of obedience that will release unprecedented blessings in your life. *"Let him who receives instruction in the Word [of God] share all good things with his teacher [contributing to his support]"* instructs **Galatians 6:6** *(*AMP). While **1Timothy 5:17** (AMP) says *"Let the elders who perform the duties of their office well be considered doubly worthy of honour [and of adequate financial support], especially those who labour faithfully in preaching and teaching"*

These scriptures refer to leaders within the church. It clearly specifies that they should be viewed worthy of not just honour but double honour. In other words, we should give unto them what is due (suitable rewards). *"Render therefore to all their dues: tribute to whom tribute is due; custom to whom custom; fear to whom fear; honour to whom honour"(* **Romans 13:7 KJV).**

Ministers often travel all over the world preaching, teaching, ministering God's healing power and delivering souls for God's kingdom and at the end of each service you may have a "spirit-filled" congregation who might never minister to the temporal needs of the preacher. This certainly does not line up with the principles of the word of the Lord. As **1Corinthians 9:13 &14** reminds us:

> *Don't you realize that those who work at the temple get their food from the temple? Don't those who help at the altar get a share of what is on the altar? In the same way, the Lord has commanded that those who spread the Good News should earn their living from the Good News*

Acts 28:10 also demonstrates how the people honoured Paul and others for healing and deliverance that they received. The people had 'laden' the ministers with gifts so that there was no lack.

I recall receiving an invitation to preach in Montego Bay, a town about a three hours drive from where I lived. It was a "wilderness" or financially challenging period for me and I had to borrow money for traveling. After ministering I received an "honorarium" which could not cover the cost of gas needed to return home and repay the sum I had borrowed.

On another occasion, I ministered at a church (not having food at home or gas in my vehicle). It was a powerful meeting. I tell you this, my friend, when I was through they stretched their hands toward me and shouted "Bless him Jesus! Bless him!" I interceded all the way home for the Holy Spirit to sustain me. Thank God the Holy Spirit came through for me as the car was not fueled by gasoline that day but by the Holy Ghost! Hallelujah! Haha haha. I laugh now, but back then....it was hard. Brethren this is not biblical as is evident from the scriptures given.

This may be the reason many Ministers go to the extreme of requesting an exorbitant honorarium. **1 Corinthians 9:18** states *"what is my reward then? Verily that, when I preach the gospel, I may make the gospel of Christ without charge, that I abuse not my power in the gospel."* What then should be the balance?

The minister should not abuse his power and the church should not abuse the minister. Paul said that everyone should give as God has prospered him (**1Cor 16:2**). This scripture clearly suggests that the capability of everyone varies. Ministers should not expect the same courtesy from every ministry because all ministries are not at the same level in their resources.

It is believed that there are many persons whose motive for being in ministry is quite questionable but *"let the wheat and the tear grow together until the day of harvest"* (**Matthew 13:30**). On the other hand the exorbitant honorarium requested by these ministers may speak to a lack of understanding on their part and not necessarily an impure motive.

There have been cases where itinerant ministers have ministered in local churches, take all the offering and leave the church in debt. Friend, this ought not to be! I cannot overemphasis the need for ministers not to abuse their power and for the church not to abuse ministers. **Philippians 4:14-16** states:

> *Notwithstanding ye have done well, that ye did communicate with my affliction. Now ye Philippians know also, that in the beginning of the gospel, when I departed from Macedonia, no church communicated with me as concerning giving and receiving, but ye only. For even in Thessalonica ye sent once and again unto my necessity.*

Why is it that the church at Philippi was the only church that gave to the Apostle Paul when he began in the ministry? Could it be that the others weren't taught the importance of giving as yet? Maybe they thought that God would physically come down and do it. I'm not sure, but one thing I do know: whenever a ministry makes a sacrifice to honour a servant of God, the principle of **Philippians 4:19** comes into play wherein *".. my God shall supply all your needs according to his riches in glory by Christ Jesus."*

Most Christians enjoy quoting and claiming this promise, but this promise is for Christians who have been supporting the work of the Lord. That is why it was written to the church at Philippi and not another. The promises of God are conditional and therefore you need to carry out your part for it to take effect. **Acts 28:9-10** (KJV) states: *"So when this was done, others also, which had diseases in the island came and were healed who also honoured us with many honours; and when we departed, they laded us with such things as were necessary."*

When you give something to a man or woman of God you are honouring them by being obedient to

God and really setting the stage for God to bless you!!!

- **God Wants Your Best**

Malachi 1:6-8 (KJV) states:

> *A son honoureth his father, and a servant his master: if then I be a father, where is mine honour? and if I be a master, where is my fear? saith the LORD of hosts unto you, O priests, that despise my name. And ye say, Wherein have we despised thy name? Ye offer polluted bread upon mine altar; and ye say, wherein have we polluted thee? In that ye say, The table of the LORD is contemptible. And if ye offer the blind for sacrifice, is it not evil? and if ye offer the lame and sick, is it not evil? offer it now unto thy governor; will he be pleased with thee, or accept thy person? saith the LORD of hosts.*

The message found in this scripture is telling us that if we are giving to God, it should be something without defect; something good enough that we would want it for ourselves. Polluted bread as mentioned in the passage, describes gifts which are unworthy to give unto the Lord.

It must be established that giving the best is the way to go when honouring God. When we give to the church or to God's representatives (pastors, ministers and their spouses) by extension we are giving to the Lord so we should also give to them our best.

Years ago I heard of this man who wanted to give something to his church. "Pastor," he called, "I just purchased a brand new couch and I want to give this old one to the church." The pastor said the thing was so old and deplorable that not even his dog would use it for a bed. Friends, that's not honouring God!

• Honour God and He Will Honour You

A few years after I started Worship and Faith International fellowship (WAFIF), I noticed that there was a great financial strain upon the ministry. This was chiefly due to the acquisition of our church property. The strain was so intense it made ministering difficult for me. Creditors were constantly calling and we were seven months in arrears with the mortgage. It was as if all hell had broken loose! I refused to accept a regular salary in an effort to keep the ministry afloat.

Amidst all this, there was a great outpouring of God's presence every week. Many went to the altar crying and requesting to be baptized. People were being healed from numerous medical conditions, varying from lumps in the breast to a brand new heart being implanted supernaturally. A little girl was also miraculously healed of scoliosis. The miracles are too numerous to remember.

Despite this, the finances were seemingly drying up and the bills continued coming. Friends, it was one of the most difficult and confusing times of my life. I would minister to people and God would release supernatural financial miracles - money showing up in accounts, debts being canceled or drastically reduced - yet I was broke! I was barely making it each day.

For more than a year I prayed, cried, and fasted for a financial release but nothing happened. One day an overpowering thought came to me, "Why don't you MIGRATE"! Friends that was the devil! I looked and saw the souls and all that God was doing at Worship and Faith International fellowship and I said "Oh no! How can I leave the babies in Christ? How many will end up in hell if I go?" Woe is me if I preach not the gospel! But how do I get out from under this pressure that is affecting me?

So I asked God the billion dollar question: "God! What do you want me to do?" Right there He showed me the rich young ruler and said, "Give me everything." I asked in disbelief, "Everything!? He said, "Yes, everything. Sell your car and your land and give the money to the church." I was amazed nevertheless I surrendered everything to God but it was *not* easy. Can you imagine how my wife felt? I know I was distraught. I cried and prayed about it for days. I felt that I had given so much already and now the two things that my wife and I had achieved, God wanted. Friends, I imagine that was how Abraham felt when he was asked to give up his son. There are some things which God requires of us that literally brings tears to our eyes but the scripture says *"They who sow in tears shall reap in joy"* **(Psalm 126:5).**

Knowledge of the word made surrendering to God easier. I recommend, therefore that believers become intimately familiar with the word of God so when tests like this comes along we have something to stand on. The moment I surrendered in my heart, even before the items were sold, the blessings started to flow as never before: supernatural wisdom was released upon me, within three months the church's mortgage which had been in arrears was almost cleared, and we were able to bring the bills up to date. People were just showing up and blessing us in various ways – honouring us with their gifts. Hallelujah! I could go on and on but suffice it to sat it was just favour, favour, favour!!! This came about because I chose to obey God.

The land was sold and the money given to the church. We tried selling the car for over a year when it suddenly dawned on us that as was the case with Abraham and Isaac, God was merely testing us where it was concerned as several attempts to sell the car proved futile. In the end a loan was taken against the car and the money given to the church. The important thing here is that I was obedient to God. In similar manner we ought to be obedient in following the principles of God as part of honouring Him.

When we honour God and consistently put His agenda above ours, the flood gate of favour will be opened! God has now blessed my wife and I and within a year of selling the land God has helped us to begin the process of acquiring a house. Friends, despite this I know the best is yet to come as God says *"them that honour me, I will honour, and they that despise me shall be lightly esteemed"* (1 **Samuel 2:30 KJV**). What will you do? Honour God and be honoured or despise him and be left out of the promise. Friend, the decision is yours. I pray you make the right choice.

2

Honour through Giving

The topic of *giving* is usually a sore point for many Christians and other individuals. It is necessary for followers of Christ to be aware of the importance of honouring God through giving. Like many other points to be discussed, it is a *principle* which means that there are benefits to be gained from following this principle.

There are many ways we can give to God. The most talked about one is money but we can also give to God through our service, by honouring our commitments and by using our talents for the advancement of the kingdom of God. It is important that in giving we give of our best and with the right motive. Contributing to the work of God will result in a harvest of blessings.

The following is the testimony of one of the deaconesses at Worship and Faith International Fellowship (WAFIF) who honoured God by giving her time and was blessed in return.

Deaconess Stephenson and her husband had been trying to have a baby since they got married and after seven years and many miscarriages she was at her breaking point, ready to give up. She had received many prophetic words regarding having a child, but each time she conceived she would have a miscarriage.

One day the spirit of God spoke to me and told me to tell her to assist my wife who had recently given birth to a baby girl. Deaconess Stephenson, trusting me as her shepherd began serving my wife. There was no task too great or too small that she would not do – she would cook, clean, care for the baby and any other duties that would free my wife to carry out her duties as a pastor's wife. Friend, this is someone that is in a good job who never had to do this but she had a *need* that money could not supply and so she chose to be obedient.

Caring for someone else's baby while it appeared she was being denied a child - the one thing she needed - was not an easy thing for Deaconess Stephenson to do but she did it anyway. The Lord had told me that after she served and assisted with my baby she would take care of her own baby. Approximately three months after assisting with my daughter she got pregnant and this time there was no miscarriage, she carried the baby yp full term. I am the baby's godfather. Glory to God! Her miracle was connected to her serving and as she served and honoured the servant of God, God honoured her. Elisha followed Elijah around doing menial task. Timothy was a personal assistant to Paul just as Deaconess Stephenson honoured us in serving thus honouring God. Are you called to serve a man or woman of God? Helping with daily tasks will relief them so they are free to do more for the lord.

We should be willing to give of ourselves in whatever way we can. This may include simple tasks such as giving of our time, cleaning the church or greeting visitors upon arrival.

Let us now look at some other ways we can give to God.

- *Tithing*

A fundamental way of honouring God is through tithing. What is tithing? Let me begin by saying tithing is your covenant responsibility as a child of God. You are obligated to tithe. Why you may ask? It is the "gateway for the believer into covenant blessings." (**Malachi 3:8-11**).

Throughout the scriptures we see that the works of God are founded on *principles*. He outlined in the Bible certain principles that we are to abide by and if followed as laid out we will reap the blessings and not just the promises of God. This may be difficult for some persons to understand so lets look at it some more.

In the Hebrew language the word for tithe "maaser" or "maasrah," is translated tenth, or tenth part, and "apodekatoo" is the Greek word for tenth. Both words mean a payment or giving or receiving of the tenth or ten percent (10%).

The Bible clearly states that a tithe/tenth of everything belongs to God. *"And all the tithe of the land, whether of the seed of the land, or of the fruit of the tree, is the Lord's: it is holy unto the Lord."* (**Leviticus 27:30**) God said to Adam in **Genesis 2:17** all the trees in the Garden you may eat of but the tree in the middle is mine. In a similar way god has blessed us with 90 and he is saying the 10 is mine. Likewise we should not touch God's tithe.

Many persons have trouble following or adhering to this principle on the grounds that tithing is an Old Testament law. Friend, this is not so. Tithing actually began before the law. In **Genesis 14: 18-20** we see where God granted Abram victory over two kings and Abram gave tithes of the spoils to Melchizedek.

> *And Melchizedek king of Salem brought forth bread and wine: and he was the priest of the most high God. And he blessed him, and said, Blessed be Abram of the most high God, possessor of heaven and earth: And blessed be the most high God, which hath delivered thine enemies into thy hand. And he gave him tithes of all.*

Tithing was included in the law of Moses hundreds after the dispensation of Abraham. Jesus chided the Scribes and Pharisees in **Matthew 23:23** for paying tithes and neglecting the weightier matters of the law, judgment, mercy and faith. Please note that in this same passage Jesus continued by saying *"..this ought ye to have done (judgment ,mercy and faith) and not leave the other undone (tithing)."*

Friend, paying your tithe should not be left undone. When we fail to pay tithe we are taking what belongs to God and that's robbery! Many are willing to give an offering but never pay their tithe not realizing that by doing this they are short changing themselves and sabotaging their success. Have you ever taken a look at how Abram got blessed? It was *after* He released the tithe that Melchizedek *released* the blessing upon him (**Hebrews 7:6**). Without this release all Abram had were promises; promises from God.

Many Christians have promises but are yet to come into the full blessings of the Lord. The type of blessing that the Lord said He would *pour out* to those who honour Him. When we begin to honour God through tithing He will release blessings we will not have room to receive. (**Malachi 3:10c**).

Please understand that the blessing is similar to that which was upon Joseph. He had the spirit of wisdom to turn things around. If you put him at the bottom, what he had on him will always cause him to rise to the top even while in prison. It is the *empowerment to succeed*. It's like a coat of favour comparable to that which Jacob gave Joseph.

This empowerment is what every believer needs. It can only be yours if you follow the principle of God. One of the best things about our Heavenly Father is that He doesn't force any one. He leaves it up to you to be obedient after hearing. This is no attempt to get you to do what you don't want, but just to share with you the steps to the gateway of success.

Let me share another testimony with you. A member of the congregation at WAFIF in his early Christian walk was earning minimum wages from his business. After hearing the message on tithing and first fruit he began tithing. About three months later he started seeing the manifestation of his faith. He went from earning (JD)$4000 per week to (JD)$40,000 and up to (JD)$60,000 some weeks.

Malachi 3:8-11 asks:

> *Will a man rob God? Yet ye have robbed me. But ye say, Wherein have we robbed thee? In tithes and offerings. Ye are cursed with a curse: for ye have robbed me, even this whole nation. Bring ye all the tithes into the storehouse, that there may be meat in mine house, and prove me now herewith,*

saith the Lord of hosts, if I will not open you the windows of heaven, and pour you out a blessing, that there shall not be room enough to receive it. And I will rebuke the devourer for your sakes, and he shall not destroy the fruits of your ground; neither shall your vine cast her fruit before the time in the field, saith the Lord of hosts.

A few things are worthy to be highlighted from this passage:

- It's robbery not to tithe (vs 8)

- We rob God not only by withholding tithes but also by withholding offering (vs 8)

- Lack of tithing blocks the blessing and brings a curse (vs 9)

- The tithe must be taken to God's storehouse otherwise called the church. The Lord describes it as *"meat in my house"* (vs 10)

- The tithes make the local church strong. It ensures that provisions are always in the house (vs 10)

- The *"Blessing"* will be released when you tithe and you will prove God in amazing ways (vs10)

- The Lord Himself will rebuke the devourer for your sake (vs 11)

- You will walk in the manifestation and not continually miss out right at the edge of your miracle.

Now let us look at the word *devourer* in verse 11 of Malachi 3. Another word for *devourer* is *seed eater*. The word clearly says when we bring the tithe into the storehouse the Lord will rebuke the devourer or seed eater. Your offering is your seed, a seed that should generate an harvest, as in **Luke 6:38, Galatians 6:6-9 and 2Corinthians 9:10** which states *"Now he that ministereth seed to the sower both minister bread for your food, and multiply your seed sown, and increase the fruits of your righteousness"*.

You must understand that if the tithe is not released first then the seed eater or devourer will destroy your seed and there will be no harvest. Believers ought to follow the principle of tithing when their desire is to honour God. You will be shocked by the blessings that will unfold year after year.

- *Offering*

We have already established that the offering is different from the tithe. The Hebrew word **for offering is teruwmah (ter-oo-maw)** meaning: A present (as offered up), especially in sacrifice or as tribute.

There are several kinds of offering mentioned in the bible, but let me list a few:

First fruit Offering - Proverbs 3: 9 &10.

This type of offering is given when

- there is an increase in your salary. That first week, fortnight or month's <u>increase</u> should go to God.
- Your first salary upon getting a new job is your firstfruit and should be given to God. Just as Able gave the first set of animals that were born so we ought to give God our first.
- At the beginning of the year your first week's or month's salary should be given. C. S. Lewis says "when the first is given the rest will be blessed".

A couple at WAFIF in January 2011 gave their firstfruit offering and at the end of it they had nothing left for grocery. They believed in the principle of firstfruit and trusted God. God honoured their faith and gift in that shortly after they received a series of blessings from God:

- somebody showed up and said the Lord told her to take the wife grocery and meat shopping .
- the wife received a promotion that almost doubled her salary,
- the husband received a promotion.
- the year before they had lost their vehicle and they got a vehicle.

Praise be to God! Friend, I am not saying that everybody who gives will get an immediate reward like the couple above but giving works! Please note, you don't **have** to give. You **get** to give. You will not go to hell for not giving firstfruit offering but it could hinder the flow of God's blessing in your life.

- *Sacrificial Seed - 1Kings 17: 8-16.*

This is an offering given when you are in trouble. This type of offering is similar to the one given by the widow in **1Kings** who gave to Elijah and God sustained her and blessed her. A visitor to WAFIF had been trying to sell a house for over five years and within a week of sowing a seed into the ministry the house was sold.

- **Kingdom Demand** - *Exodus 25: 1-8*

When the temple was to be built God instructed Moses to "require an offering of the people". When your local church is expanding you can partner with the pastor by contributing this type of offering.

- **Thanksgiving Offering** –

This is a special offering given to God just because He has been good to you. You are not asking for anything, you are merely thanking Him for blessing you, protecting you or for any other event in your live that you can identify the hand of God at work. You are simply thanking God for undeserved blessings.

HOW SHOULD YOU GIVE?

We should give with souls in mind remembering that it is the Lord thy God *"… that giveth thee power to get wealth, that he may establish his covenant which he sware unto thy fathers, as it is this day."* **(Deuteronomy 8:18).**

When you give you should give in faith because *whatever is not of faith is sin* **(Romans 14:23)**

Give with a pure motive, with the right intentions and watch God work. You should also give freely, willing and cheerfully - God loves a cheerful giver.

Remember, this is something you **get to do** and not **have to do**.

3

Honouring the Five-fold Ministry

Ministers of the gospel are God's gift to his church. The Lord builds His body or kingdom through the five-fold ministry. As is seen in **Ephesians 4:11-12** (KJV) God states that, *"11... he gave some, apostles; and some, prophets; and some, evangelists; and some, pastors and teachers; 12For the perfecting of the saints, for the work of the ministry, for the edifying of the body of Christ."*

God has given the grace to men and women to function in each of the different ministries or offices in order to edify and mature the saints. Many of us have only been exposed to one aspect or finger of the five-fold ministry and this can negatively affect our spiritual growth.

All dimensions of the five-fold ministry should operate at the foundation of the local church. This foundation is necessary if the plan of God is to be accomplished in and through the church.

Therefore, it is very important that we know how to identify the gifts of our ministers and the role they play so that they will be appropriately positioned or placed.

Three (3) Major Purposes of the Five-fold Ministry

1. Perfecting of the Saints

This speaks to the maturing of the saints. All believers have the responsibility and freedom to receive perfection through *apostles, prophets, evangelists, pastors and teachers*. The maturing or lack thereof, of every saint affects the performance of the whole body of Christ. It comes with much work, patience and persistence. It's about hearing from God and as a leader it's about doing what's best for your flock. This requires the correct diet (word), exercise (opportunity to serve) and discipline (rebuke and correction in love).

2. Equipping Saints for the work of the ministry

Ministry is man's service done to the glory of God to direct men to Christ and in fulfilling his purpose in God. A church may be successful in evangelism but could be lacking in the other areas. A balance diet will solve this problem. When the five-fold ministry is harmoniously operating, it provides the platform for the saints to be trained and equipped to do what God wants them to do.

Ephesians 2:19-20 (KJV) states *"Now therefore ye are no more strangers and foreigners, but fellow citizens with the saints, and of the household of God; ²⁰And are built upon the foundation of the apostles and prophets, Jesus Christ himself being the chief corner stone."* While **1 Corinthians 3:9** says *"For we are labourers together with God: ye are God's husbandry, ye are God's building."*

Friends, you and I are privileged to be called to serve in the work of the Lord. We should not shrink away from the various opportunities to serve. We should make ourselves available to be trained, so that we can be used effectively. It's a major step in honoring God. You've been called to serve. Every Christian has something to offer to help build the kingdom of God. Have you found your area of service? Remember the word of God says:

> *From whom the whole body fitly joined together and compacted by that which <u>every joint supplieth</u>, according to the effectual working in the measure of every part, maketh increase of the body unto the edifying of itself in love.* **(Ephesians 4:16).**

Every joint supplieth! Wow! That includes you! You have something to offer.

3. *Edifying of the Body of Christ*

Edifying means building up. Through the five-fold ministry, the Holy Spirit builds up the whole body of Christ. The body of Christ is neither a human organization, nor a denomination. It is instead an organism, which is being built up for the Lord. The local church is a member of the universal body of Christ. It is God's plan for the Church to grow into a perfect MAN - *unto the measure of the stature of the fullness of Christ.* This simply means that a mature local church should function just as Christ functioned when He walked the earth.

As we mature, our love walk will increase and together we will flow in all the gifts of the spirit. *"Till we all come in the unity of the faith, and of the knowledge of the Son of God, unto a perfect man, unto the measure of the stature of the fullness of Christ"* **Ephesians 4:13** (KJV). Take time out and pray that these ministries flow purely in your church. I pray that the Lord will continue to rise up apostles, prophets, evangelists, pastors and teachers in our local churches.

The Role of Each Ministry

I have seen where the right hand is often used to demonstrate the role of the five-fold ministry. In the text below, the *'man's hand'* could be seen as a prophetic sign of the five-fold ministry that God would use to bring revival. *"And it came to pass at the seventh time, that he said, Behold, there ariseth a little cloud out of the sea, like a man's hand. And he said, Go up, say unto Ahab, Prepare [thy chariot], and get thee down, that the rain stop thee not"* (**1Kings 18:44**)

Let me also add that there are many ministers who flow with a combination of the gifts such as prophetic evangelist, apostolic pastors, prophetic pastors, evangelistic pastors and pastors who are excellent teachers. The apostle generally flows in all five but not at the same time. For example, Paul who was a teacher functioned as an evangelist and had the seer gift of the prophet. He was a Pastor at other times and was definitely an Apostle.

One clear sign of the apostleship is authority combined with humility and a strong flow of the miraculous. It is critically important to connect with the five-fold ministry. The grace which flows from this ministry will flow within the local church. After getting connected with our ministry many of our members gradually began flowing in the prophetic. I have also seen the birth of many dynamic preachers within our ministry operating with a strong healing gift.

Friends, this is not new or reserve for some churches. The word of God tells us that King Saul prophesied when he was in the company of the prophets.

> *And when they came thither to the hill, behold, a company of prophets met him; and*

the Spirit of God came upon him, and he prophesied among them. And it came to pass, when all that knew him beforetime saw that, behold, he prophesied among the prophets, then the people said one to another, What is this that is come unto the son of Kish? Is Saul also among the prophets? **(1Samuel 10:10-11)**

From our experience at Worship and Faith International Fellowship and the above scripture it is clear that the anointing on the leader will impact and saturate those who are truly connected.

I Kings 18:44
Ephesians 4:11

The Apostle (The Thumb)

The thumb represents the Apostle. It is the first headship of the church. The term apostle is derived from the New Testament Greek word *apostolos*, meaning one commissioned by Christ with miraculous power; one who is sent forth as a messenger. It should not be confused with an evangelist. The apostle has the right and authority to touch every member of the body of the five-fold ministry. He is a pastor to the other four. Apostleship is about laying the foundation by selecting the Pastor for a new settlement as well as Evangelism for bringing in people for new membership. They operate as missionaries.

As the Apostle Paul said in **1Corinthians 9:1-2** (KJV) *"¹Am I not an apostle? am I not free? have I not seen Jesus Christ our Lord? are not ye my work in the Lord? ²If I be not an apostle unto others, yet doubtless I am to you: for the seal of mine apostleship are ye in the Lord."*

An apostle is anointed to "establish churches". Therefore, their roles extend beyond their local boundaries. They will set up churches as well as leadership in cities, countries and nations. The Apostle incorporates the word of God as the basis of the church's existence. Apostles will provide parental support for new churches. This role may reduce over time. One of my dear friends and brother in the ministry Prophet Michael Carter wrote that "Apostles govern. They are the chief governing officer of the church."(SOURCE)

The Prophet (The Second/Pointer Finger)

A prophet is a spokesperson for God. The Hebrew word for prophet is *'nabiy'* meaning an inspired man who speaks on God's behalf while the Greek word for prophet is *'prophetes'*, which means foreteller. The prophet has the grace to admonish, warn, direct, encourage, intercede, teach and counsel based on his revelatory gifts. *Acts: 21 10 & 11* says

> *And as we tarried there many days, there came down from Judaea a certain prophet, named Agabus. And when he was come unto us, he took Paul's girdle, and bound his own hands and feet, and said, Thus saith the Holy Ghost, So shall the Jews at Jerusalem bind the man that owneth this girdle, and shall deliver him into the hands of the Gentiles.*

In the above scripture the prophet Agabus told Paul what would happen. Sometimes the prophetic word will be for the church as a whole or for the leadership of the church. **Amos 3:7** (KJV) tells us that *"Surely the Lord GOD will do nothing, but he revealeth his secret unto his servants the prophets."*

In the Old Testament, the people feared the prophets, knowing that they were messengers from God who usually brought words of correction. **Jeremiah 1:9-10** (KJV) *"Then the LORD put forth his hand, and touched my mouth. And the LORD said unto me, Behold, I have put my words in thy mouth. See, I have this day set thee over the nations and over the kingdoms, to root out, and to pull down, and to destroy, and to throw down, to build, and to plant."*

In the New Testament we see where the purpose of a prophecy is three-fold – it comforts, edifies and it exhorts. **1Corinthians 14:3** (KJV) explains that *"...he that prophesieth speaketh unto men to edification, and exhortation, and comfort."* I know individuals who have received prophetic words that have not yet come to pass and as a result they have shut down their spirits. They are no longer open to the prophetic. But **1Thessalonians 5:20-21** says *"despise not prophesyings. Prove all things; hold fast that which is good."*

Prophet Michael Carter has been a tremendous blessing to the Worship and Faith International Fellowship (WAFIF) family. Through his prophetic ministry several members of the congregation have received accurate word of knowledge and clear cut prophetic words that have brought great comfort and peace in seasons of turmoil. This was only possible because they chose to believe the prophet.

I have also seen where God has used me to give accurate prophetic words which brought great comfort to many. I share the following testimony with the permission of one of my spiritual daughters, Delcita. God gave me a word for her years ago stating that she would be promoted in three months. Friends, in exactly three months a position was created for her which also gave her a significant salary increase. You might ask why would God do or say that. You see, she needed a financial breakthrough and that word came to encourage her in a time when she needed it. To Him belong the glory and the praise!

That's not all friends. Right after she was promoted God gave me another word that there would be another promotion within a few months and God did it. Glory to God! Prophets are not only relevant but they are real and they exist today! Pray that God would increase His prophetic anointing among your ministers so that you too can be edified, encouraged and comforted in your journey to honouring God.

The Evangelist (Third/The Middle Finger)

The third finger represents the *evangelist*. Holding your hand out flat and fingers together, you will find your middle finger is the longest finger on your hand. This finger sticks out more than the other four. In the same breath, an evangelist goes into communities to bring souls to the kingdom of God. Preaching is the central work of an evangelist.

The word "evangelist" comes from the Greek word, *euaggelistes*, which means a preacher of the Gospel. The Bible more often uses the word evangelist to describe someone who has given up secular work and devote their profession to that of proclaiming Christ in an effort to bring men to God.

Evangelists are generally itinerant preachers. They usually travel to churches, conventions and crusades at the invitation of host pastors to share the word of God with one objective - to pull men to Christ. They also host street meetings as Phillip did in **Act 8: 5**: *"Then Philip went down to the city of Samaria, and preached Christ unto them."* The strength of the evangelist is in God's grace operating through him to accomplish this task.

The Pastor (The Fourth/Ring Finger)

The fourth finger, the *ring finger* or the *covenant finger,* represents the Pastor of the church. The pastor is married to the church. He or she is in covenant with the church that God has placed him over. The pastor is the set man and spiritual father of the house.

As I speak of the five-fold ministry, it is necessary for me to add that God always calls a man or woman and then gives them a vision that is bigger than they are. He then sends people to undergird that leader. There should be no confusion here: although you are called to undergird or complement the pastor, you must know and respect his position. A part of honouring God is being submissive to those He has placed over you irrespective of who you are.

God had called Moses to lead the Israelites out of captivity. He gave Aaron and Miriam the responsibility of assisting Moses. They were ministers but had to understand and exercise respect for God's set man – Moses. The moment they began to undermine and criticize Moses, leprosy broke out on Miriam. Aaron was however protected by his priestly garment. As soon as that garment was removed he died. The story can be found in Numbers 12:1-10.

> *¹And Miriam and Aaron spake against Moses because of the Ethiopian woman whom he had married: for he had married an Ethiopian woman.²And they said, Hath the LORD indeed spoken only by Moses? hath he not spoken also by us? And the LORD heard it.³(Now the man Moses was very meek, above all the men which were upon the face of the earth.)⁴And the LORD spake suddenly unto Moses, and unto Aaron, and unto Miriam, Come out ye three unto the tabernacle of the congregation. And they three came out.⁵And the LORD came down in the pillar of the cloud, and stood in the door of the tabernacle, and called Aaron and Miriam: and they both came forth.⁶And he said, Hear now my words: If there be a*

prophet among you, I the LORD will make myself known unto him in a vision, and will speak unto him in a dream.[7]My servant Moses is not so, who is faithful in all mine house.[8]With him will I speak mouth to mouth, even apparently, and not in dark speeches; and the similitude of the LORD shall he behold: wherefore then were ye not afraid to speak against my servant Moses?[9]And the anger of the LORD was kindled against them; and he departed.[10]And the cloud departed from off the tabernacle; and, behold, Miriam became leprous, white as snow: and Aaron looked upon Miriam, and, behold, she was leprous.

Never touch the Lord's anointed! **In 1Samuel 24:2-10** David could have killed Saul many times but he didn't because he was the Lord's anointed.

Then Saul took three thousand chosen men out of all Israel, and went to seek David and his men upon the rocks of the wild goats. [3]And he came to the sheepfold by the way, where was a cave; and Saul went in to cover his feet: and David and his men remained in the sides of the cave.[4]And the men of David said unto him, Behold the day of which the LORD said unto thee, Behold, I will deliver thine enemy into thine hand, that thou mayest do to him as it shall seem good unto thee. Then David arose, and cut off the skirt of Saul's robe privily.[5]And it came to pass afterward, that David's heart smote him, because he had cut off Saul's skirt.[6]And he said unto his men, The LORD forbid that I should do this thing unto my master, the LORD's anointed, to stretch forth mine hand against him, seeing he is the anointed of the LORD.[7]So David stayed his servants with these words, and suffered them not to rise against Saul. But Saul rose up out of the cave, and went on his way.[8]David also arose afterward, and went out of the cave, and cried after Saul, saying, My lord the king. And when Saul looked behind him, David stooped with his face to the earth, and bowed himself.[9]And David said to Saul, Wherefore hearest thou men's words, saying, Behold, David seeketh thy hurt?[10]Behold, this day thine eyes have seen how that the LORD had delivered thee to day into mine hand in the cave: and some bade me kill thee: but mine eye spared thee; and I said, I will not put forth mine hand against my lord; for he is the LORD's anointed.

In a similar way we should not touch the Lord's anointed. The Bible says *"Rebuke not an elder, but* entreat him as a father; and the younger men as brethren" (**1Timothy 5:1**). It is inappropriate, therefore, for members to criticize and rebuke their leaders. God has a system to bring correction to His leaders. Every pastor should have an apostle or someone at their level that has the freedom to speak into his or her life, be it a correction, rebuke or reproof. Paul had the authority as an apostle to rebuke Peter and he did. Miriam and Aaron were out of order as subordinates to rebuke Moses. Friends, if our intention is to honour God, we need to learn the little nuances that are involved in the process and respecting and honouring our pastor is a critical first step to know.

The pastor provides meat for the church. He preaches the word to teach the flock of God - **Jeremiah 3:15** (KJV) *"And I will give you pastors according to mine heart, which shall feed you with knowledge and understanding."* **Jeremiah 23:4** (KJV) says *"And I will set up shepherds over them which shall feed them: and they shall fear no more, nor be dismayed, neither shall they be lacking, saith the LORD."*

The pastor, as the spiritual father should mentor and then release others. I served in a certain ministry for many years. One day I had some differences with my local superior. It got really uncomfortable. I was rebuked before the congregation. My flesh wanted to retaliate but how could I touch the Lord's anointed? I humbled myself. You see, the Lord says, *if we humble ourselves we will be exalted* (**Luke 14:11**).

When my superior was through, I offered him a glass of water as a servant would a master. As a result of my respect for authority, coupled with the fact that my heart was right before the Lord, God allowed the Bishop of that organization to release me with a blessing when the time came for me to leave that organization.

The role of the pastor is quite comprehensive. He teaches, preaches, counsels and is always praying for the church. He fathers the fatherless and knows that he is a role-model in and out of the church's environment. He is the shepherd who keeps his sheep from wandering off; he is responsible for each sheep within his flock - *"Woe be unto the pastors that destroy and scatter the sheep of my pasture! saith the LORD."* **(Jeremiah 23:1, KJV***).*

I've known of "pastors" who seek to manipulate and abuse the sheep. I remember one pastor pronouncing curses over members who decided to leave his ministry. Friends, this is not scriptural so flee from those who are seeking to control your life! It is critically important that you know to whom God has connected you. The wrong connection or the wrong house could make your walk and your progress with God stagnant and may even hinder your advancement in life.

The Teacher (The Fifth/Pinkie Finger)

The fifth and final finger on the hand is called the *"pinkie"* finger. It plays the role of the teacher. It is the smallest finger and in most cases it has the hardest job. The teacher is anointed to bring the word of God with clarity and substance. A teacher is an establisher and a strengthener. He is an establisher in rooting and grounding people in the word of God, in the truths of the Bible, so that they can stand the attacks of Satan and walk in faith.

A dedicated teacher studies and prepares for challenges which may arise among the flock. **Romans 12:2** states *"And be not conformed to this world: but be ye transformed by the renewing of your mind, that ye may prove what is that good, and acceptable, and perfect, will of God."*

A teacher should teach with a "pastor's heart". That is, with genuine concern for the spiritual development of each member so that they will know how to survive in the world. **Isaiah 28**:9-10 says *"Whom shall he teach knowledge? and whom shall he make to understand doctrine? them that are weaned from the milk, and drawn from the breasts. For precept must be upon precept, precept upon precept; line upon line, line upon line; here a little, and there a little."*

A word of caution, I know of many persons who will not readily sit and listen to a teacher, saying "it's boring." That's dishonourable! What we need is balance and an understanding that all the gifts are needed to establish us. The teacher informs and instructs while the preacher inspires and stirs. To

HONOURING THE FIVE-FOLD MINISTRY

disrespect is to dishonour! To disregard and not place value on the gift is definitely dishonourable!

Years ago, when I just started out in the ministry, my pastor invited a guest speaker. As he began to share, I said to myself, "man this guy is boring!" I then remembered that everyone's flow or style of presentation is different so I took out my notepad and began taking notes. Wow! I was so blessed by the information he gave. God really spoke to me through that speaker. It was as if he had given me more than the presenter delivered.

We must be careful of self proclaimed apostles, evangelist, prophets, pastors and teachers. David was not a self proclaimed "king". He was released by the prophet Samuel. The apostle Paul had set Timothy over certain churches making him the set man. Hands were laid on Timothy and then he was released. Children of God, were you released in similar fashion in leaving your parent church to start your own ministry or to attend another church? Or did you just up and leave? It so I encourage you to go back and make amends with your spiritual father so that you can come into all that God has in store for you.

55

The responsibility of each person in the Five-Fold ministry was summarized by Prophet Michael Carter in his book "Don't give up on the Church", beautifully. He said that the *apostle governs, the prophet guides, the pastor guards, the evangelist gathers and the teacher...*

4

Honouring Your Pastor

The Other Side

Many would wonder why pastors need to be in full time ministry. The bottom line is, being a minister of a church is a lot of work but most of the work takes place behind the scene. Some of the pastor's responsibilities include preparing messages, praying for and counseling members and visitors, conducting weddings, funerals, administrating and planning for the growth of the ministry to name a few. Remember what Jesus told Martha in **Luke 10: 41- 42**, *"And Jesus answered and said unto her, Martha, Martha, thou art careful and troubled about many things: [42]But one thing is needful: and Mary hath chosen that good part, which shall not be taken away from her."*

In **Acts 6:4** Peter exemplified or set the example for what the priority of the minister ought to be. *"But we will give ourselves continually to prayer, and to the ministry of the word."* This means praying and preaching or teaching the word of God should be the priority of the pastor. Ministers sometimes get caught up or overwhelm with other aspects of their job that they neglect this most important part. I believe that at least fifty percent (50%) of the minister's work time should be spent in the word and in prayer as this will make his ministry effective. A praying minister is able to labour effectively in preaching the gospel after spending hours in prayer and studying the word of God. It is this kind of labour and sacrifice that makes the man of God worthy to be honoured by his congregation.

Worshiping or Honouring?

I've seen where congregations who seek to honour their leaders be accused of worshipping them. But Friends, there is a difference. When you publicly acknowledge the labour and sacrifice of your man of God and show your appreciation for his faithfulness, you should give honour and not worship. This is accomplished when it is done in a manner which applauses the sacrifice of the minister while giving God the glory for all that has been achieved.

People should never get jealous or indignant when leaders are acknowledged or praised for their hard work. God is expecting us to praise each other! I know this may seem strange to you but it's biblical. *"Let another and not thine own lips praise thee"* says **Proverbs 27:2.** To praise is to *admire, to commend, to honour or to pay tribute to.* Friends, it is important to show appreciation where it is due as the bible says *"Render to Caesar the things that are Caesar's..."* (**Mark 12:17**). If your pastor or other ministers are deserving of appreciation and praise why not give it?

Every year companies carry out an appraisal of their staff. If given a high rating, employees are honoured in various ways depending on the culture of the organization. In the same manner churches are to reward their ministers according to their ability. As a leader, I know how I feel when appreciation is expressed. When this happens I give all the glory to God. As the songwriter pens: *"...for all that I am, and ever hope to be, I owe it all to thee...to God be the glory."* When was the last time you honour your pastor?

Honouring is a two way street. As leaders we should also acknowledge our staff or those who have made sacrifices to facilitate success within our ministry or on a project. My assistant had an anniversary and wanted to carry out his wife but I knew he never had the resources. My wife and I decided to finance their second "honeymoon" by making reservation at a nice hotel for them. This was a sacrifice for us but Friends, as a result of these little things my ministers are faithful servants in the kingdom who I can call upon at any time. They know that as their leader I appreciate them and I not only say it but I also show it.

Many Christians are happy to call their pastors and other ministers their spiritual parents and often seek them out for prayer, for counseling when they need a spiritual advisor, for guidance, for love and even for the bond they had or lack with their biological parents. However, when it is their birthday, Mother's Day or Father's Day these men and women of God are barely recognized for their role in the spiritual development and growth of these 'children'. Many might not have given birth to children biologically, but spiritually they have nurtured many as Paul noted in **Galatians 4:19**

"My little children, of whom I travail in birth again until Christ be formed in you" Take every opportunity to make them feel honoured as a spiritual parent. There is always a blessing to obtain when we honour the man or woman of God.

Head First

Honour flows from the head down. Remember, as you honour your leaders (the head), the blessing will flow down to you. **Psalm 133:1-3** reads:

> *"¹Behold, how good and how pleasant it is for brethren to dwell together in unity! ²It is like the precious ointment upon the head, that ran down upon the beard, even Aaron's beard: that went down to the skirts of his garments; ³As the dew of Hermon, and as the dew that descended upon the mountains of Zion: for there the LORD commanded the blessing, even life for evermore."*

This is a promise God has made. As He blesses the leader of the house the other occupants will also be blessed. Remember you are not in competition with your head. You want the favour and grace to increase upon him! You want the anointing to increase and overflow in his life! The overflow will gush down to you and prosperity will increase if you remain connected to the head – your spiritual leader.

Catching the Spirit of the House

Every church flows differently. If you are in a situation where you have recently changed your house of worship and you strongly believe that God has connected you to this new house, seek to catch the spirit of the house, (i.e. learn how your new church operates). It is quite unlikely that this new church will function like your old church. Avoid comparing and seeking to transform your new church into your old church. This is important to keep the connection with the head. The quicker you come on board with how the house flows the more readily you will see the blessings of the Lord in your life.

TWELVE WAYS TO HONOUR YOUR PASTORS

The Godly character, work and position of your pastor as one who is called and ordained to the office of pastor and shepherd make him worthy of honour. To make serving and honouring him easy, please consider the following points:

1. *Partner with your Pastor*

Partner with your pastor for the fulfillment of the vision that God has placed in his heart. Flow with your pastor's vision and do all you can to avoid injecting another stream into this vision. *"And the LORD said, Behold, the people is one, and they have all one language; and this they begin to do: and now nothing will be restrained from them, which they have imagined to do."* **Genesis 11:6**.

There are four things that stand out in this text:
- they were one,
- they had one language,
- they were doing and
- nothing would be restrained from them what they imagined to do.

Can you imagine what would happen in a church if you partner with your pastor in this way? If the entire congregation comes together in this way we would turn the nation right side! Nothing would be restrained! Whatever duties you are asked to perform in the ministry, do so without murmuring; do it as best as you can. Be submissive, obeying with the right attitude. *"Do all things without murmurings and disputing: That ye may be blameless and harmless, the sons of God, without rebuke, in the midst of a crooked and perverse nation, among whom ye shine as lights in the world."* (**Philippians 2:14-15,** KJV)

2. *See Your Pastor as God's Gift to You*

When you are connected to the right spiritual leader, you will find that pastor to be unique. God made him or her different from any other pastor you have ever known and will ever know. Avoid comparing him or her with other pastors; avoid criticizing them. **1Thessalonians 5:12-13** says *"Recognize those who labour among you, and are over you in the Lord and admonish you, and to esteem them very highly in love for their work's sake."* See them for the gift they are to you, both spiritually and otherwise.

Hebrews 13:7 also says *"Remember your leaders who first taught you the word of God. Think of all the good that has come from their lives, and trust the Lord as they do"* (New Living Translation). Isn't your man of God following Jesus Christ as set forth in the word of God? Hasn't your man or woman of God been a good example of what Christ desires of His children? If so, that my friend is a gift!

If there is a legitimate matter that concerns your pastor or any leader in the church, it should be addressed as set out in the Bible. In **1 Timothy 5:19** the Apostle Paul said, *"Do not receive an accusation against an elder except from two or three witnesses."* You may make an appointment and express your concerns. Criticism behind your pastor's back doesn't help anyone. It can certainly cause a lot of harm to your pastor's reputation and to the flow of the anointing in the house. Think of a child's behaviour on Christmas morning upon receiving a wanted gift and give your pastor that honour by receiving him in that manner every time he comes to you – a treasured gift!!

3. *Respect, Honour and receive your Pastor's Spouse*

Avoid comparing your Pastor's spouse with anyone else. God made them differently and anointed each to stand with the man or woman of God placed over you. Look at what happened to Miriam as she criticized Moses for marrying an Ethiopian woman. **Numbers 12: 1- 16** states:

> *¹And Miriam and Aaron spake against Moses because of the Ethiopian woman whom he had married: for he had married an Ethiopian woman. ²And they said, Hath the LORD indeed spoken only by Moses? hath he not spoken also by us? And the LORD heard it .³(Now the man Moses was very meek, above all the men which were upon the face of the earth.) ⁴And the LORD spake suddenly unto Moses, and unto Aaron, and unto Miriam, Come out ye three unto the tabernacle of the congregation. And they three came out .⁵And the LORD came down in the pillar of the cloud, and stood in the door of the tabernacle, and called Aaron and Miriam: and they both came forth .⁶And he said, Hear now my words: If there be a prophet among you, I the LORD will make myself known unto him in a vision, and will speak unto him in a dream .⁷My servant Moses is not so, who is faithful in all mine*

house .⁸With him will I speak mouth to mouth, even apparently, and not in dark speeches; and the similitude of the LORD shall he behold: wherefore then were ye not afraid to speak against my servant Moses? ⁹And the anger of the LORD was kindled against them; and he departed. ¹⁰And the cloud departed from off the tabernacle; and, behold, Miriam became leprous, white as snow: and Aaron looked upon Miriam, and, behold, she was leprous .¹¹And Aaron said unto Moses, Alas, my lord, I beseech thee, lay not the sin upon us, wherein we have done foolishly, and wherein we have sinned. ¹²Let her not be as one dead, of whom the flesh is half consumed when he cometh out of his mother's womb. ¹³And Moses cried unto the LORD, saying, Heal her now, O God, I beseech thee. ¹⁴And the LORD said unto Moses, If her father had but spit in her face, should she not be ashamed seven days? let her be shut out from the camp seven days, and after that let her be received in again. ¹⁵And Miriam was shut out from the camp seven days: and the people journeyed not till Miriam was brought in again.

Friends, it's not an honourable thing to speak ill of God's servant. Let us hold up our pastor's family in fervent prayer every day. Let us seek to encourage them often and let us have the courage to stand up for them whenever anyone seeks to tear them down. It's very difficult being a minister's spouse. Pray! Pray! Pray!

4. *Develop and Transform yourself with the Information you receive*

Once you have found the pastor and church to which you are connected spiritual growth must be evident. Invest in CDs, books and DVDs of the ministry (if available), take notes as your pastor speaks and avoid a "know it all" attitude; be open to hear and learn so that you can be doers of the word and grow spiritually. Follow your pastor's examples as they follow Christ and you will begin to flow in a similar anointing as you trust the Lord.

One of the most frustrating things for leaders is to be pouring out their hearts to a congregation who does not meditate on the teachings in an effort to be transformed. You give honour to the man and woman of God when they are able to see your spiritual growth. When you value the messages, this will cause you to receive knowledge that will help you to move closer to the next dimension,

towards your destiny; from glory to glory, from
wealth to wealth and from faith to faith.

5. *Avoid Familiarity*

Do not allow the spirit of familiarity to cloud your
mind and erase the boundary between you and
your man and woman of God. Show respect to
your leader's authority by addressing them as
"Pastor" rather than simply by their first name. We
should also avoid nodding our head in response to
our pastor. Give clear answers: *yes sir; no sir or
end with the person's title.* For example: *Yes
pastor; No pastor* etc. If being instructed on a
subject, write down the instructions to show you
value what is being said. This will also help you
carry out the instructions thoroughly later on.

Familiarity will block the flow of the anointing and
prevent its effectiveness in your life. Jesus couldn't
do many miracles in his own town because the
people allowed familiarity to block the flow.
Matthew 13:54-58 tells this story clearly.

> [54]*And when he was come into his own
> country, he taught them in their synagogue,
> insomuch that they were astonished, and
> said, Whence hath this man this wisdom,*

> and these mighty works? [55]*Is not this the carpenter's son? is not his mother called Mary? and his brethren, James, and Joses, and Simon, and Judas?* [56]*And his sisters, are they not all with us? Whence then hath this man all these things?* [57]*And they were offended in him. But Jesus said unto them, A prophet is not without honour, save in his own country, and in his own house.* [58]*And he did not many mighty works there because of their unbelief.*

The spirit of familiarity among the people caused unbelief and dishonour. The disciple's familiarity with Jesus also caused them not to see the importance of the woman honouring Christ when she gave Him her most treasured and expensive gift as told in **Matthew 26:7-10.**

> [7]*There came unto him a woman having an alabaster box of very precious ointment, and poured it on his head, as he sat at meat.* [8]*But when his disciples saw it, they had indignation, saying, To what purpose is this waste?* [9]*For this ointment might have been sold for much, and given to the poor.* [10]*When Jesus understood it, he said unto them, Why trouble ye the woman? for she*

hath wrought a good work upon me.

Examine your relationship with your man or woman of God. Does it reek of familiarity? Have the lines of demarcation been erased? If your desire is to honour God and see the ministry grow, you need to repair this as soon as possible. This can be done in a number of ways – open confession in church, personal letter of apology to you pastor or a card. The method is not important. What is significant is the obedience.

6. Honour your Pastors with your Gifts

A gift is not an obligation but there are blessings associated with giving gifts with the correct motive. You may not have much to offer your pastor or you may even believe deep within that they are not in need of the little you have. But remember that giving to them brings great benefit to you.

"⁶Let him that is taught in the word communicate unto him that teacheth in all good things. ⁷ Be not deceived; God is not mocked: for whatsoever a man soweth, that shall he also reap. For he that soweth to his flesh shall of the flesh reap corruption; but

*he that soweth to the Spirit shall of the Spirit reap life everlasting." (***Galatians 6:6-8***)*

The emphasis is not on what or how much you give but in the fact that you give as you are able to. The widow who gave two small coins was noticed by Jesus and He said she actually gave more because she gave out of nothing **(Mark 12:42-44)**. Everyone can give something but it takes faithfulness. As we saw in the story with the woman and her alabaster box, she continued to give her best despite the objections of others including those close to Jesus. **Galatians 6:9** encourages us to *not be weary in well doing: for in due season we shall reap, if we faint not"*

7. Pray for Your Leaders

Pray for your pastor every day. Ask God to bless your pastor with an abundance of love, hope, joy, faith, peace, power, wisdom, and courage. As Paul wrote in **2Thessalonian 3:1-2** *"Finally, brethren, pray for us, that the word of the Lord may run swiftly and be glorified, just as it is with you, and that we may be delivered from unreasonable and wicked men; for not all have faith."*

We should not under estimate the impact of the prayers of the Christians on Paul's ministry. It is clear that through the prayers of the churches at Ephesus, Colossae and Thessalonica he received much aid in preaching the word of God. He would have been left without this spiritual shield had the church failed to pray for him.

I believe Peter's deliverance from prison and death was due to the prayers of the church as recounted in **Act 12:3 -11**:

> *³And because he saw it pleased the Jews; he proceeded further to take Peter also* (These were the days of unleavened bread).*⁴And when he had apprehended him, he put him in prison, and delivered him to four quaternions of soldiers to keep him; intending after Easter to bring him forth to the people.⁵Peter therefore was kept in prison: but prayer was made without ceasing of the church unto God for him. ⁶And when Herod would have brought him forth, the same night Peter was sleeping between two soldiers, bound with two chains: and the keepers before the door kept the prison.⁷And, behold, the angel of the*

Lord came upon him, and a light shined in the prison: and he smote Peter on the side, and raised him up, saying, Arise up quickly. And his chains fell off from his hands. ⁸And the angel said unto him, Gird thyself, and bind on thy sandals. And so he did. And he saith unto him, Cast thy garment about thee, and follow me.⁹And he went out, and followed him; and wist not that it was true which was done by the angel; but thought he saw a vision.¹⁰When they were past the first and the second ward, they came unto the iron gate that leadeth unto the city; which opened to them of his own accord: and they went out, and passed on through one street; and forthwith the angel departed from him. ¹¹And when Peter was come to himself, he said, Now I know of a surety, that the Lord hath sent his angel, and hath delivered me out of the hand of Herod, and from all the expectation of the people of the Jews.

As Christians, we need to understand that praying for our leaders is one of the greatest gifts we could ever give. We have started a culture in our church recently where members are asked to fast and pray for all the ministers and their families on a particular day. Participation in such a fast shows your support for their work. So Pray! Pray! Pray!

8. Stay Connected with your Pastor

Elisha needed his connection with Elijah, Ruth needed her connection with Naomi, Timothy needed the connection with the Apostle Paul and similarly, you need your connection with the anointed servant of God who is set over you. A blender can do a lot of things but is of no use if not connected to the power that enables it to function. When God connects you to a man or woman of God, the devil will most definitely try to destroy that connection.

The enemy will aim to use five (5) things to destroy your connection:

a) *Gossip* – Do not allow people to walk up to you and carelessly tell you things they have heard about your leader (without responsible witnesses)

b) *Slander* – When the connection is created by God, the enemy will try to put dirt into your well to block your flow. Do not allow the enemy to use you to smear or defame the character of your pastor – hear no evil and speak no evil. The word of God says *"Whoso privily slandereth his neighbour, him will I cut off:..."* **(Psalm 101:5)**

c) *Fault Finding* – Do not be distracted by the wrong things. Ask God to search you to find if you have a critical spirit. You should look for the "good" in everything before searching for the "bad". Your man of God may not be as strong or eloquent as you think he ought to be but know that God generally uses the weak things of this world to confound the strong and wise **(1Corinthians 1:27).**

d) *Accusation* – David did not seek to judge Saul, he allowed God to judge him. The devil is the accuser of the brethren; don't take the devil's job.

e) *Offense* - This will be one of the biggest strategies of the enemy! Offense is also a blessing blocker! *"Blessed is he, whosoever shall not be offended in me"* (**Matthew 11:6**). When you take on offense it will block the flow of blessing from the leader to you. The word offense literally means entrapment. It will entrap you. We've got to learn to let things go. *"Judge not, and ye shall not be judged: condemn not, and ye shall not be condemned: forgive, and ye shall be forgiven"* **Luke 6:37** (KJV).

Opportunities to take offense are all around. It's up to us to determine what we are going to do: take offense and break the connection or let it go and reap the reward.

There are numerous testimonies from within our ministry where members have shared how their lives were transformed as a result of being connected. The following is a powerful testimony of how a couple's life was restored, which they dubbed "A new beginning", once they were connected to the right house.

"My husband Kayson, my daughter Abida and I walked through the doors of Worship and Faith International Fellowship broke and in debt. Our marriage was so broken down we were thinking of a divorce. Our living condition was really messy, we were knocked out of the race, our entire life was in chaos and we had no fight left in us.

Our first visit was like nothing we had ever experienced. We were greeted with love and warmth. The atmosphere was electrifying and the word when spoken by the man of God, lifted our faith so much that we decided to sow a seed for our marriage, our finances, and life overall. Miraculously, within a week we saw a turnaround.

Our lives have completely changed! We are seeing blessings in every way. My husband has received over seven (7) salary increases; we have received countless healings and deliverances; I was given gifts in the form of clothing and shoes; we began building our own home; our mindset has changed for the better as a result of a powerful series "Redefining Myself", taught by Pastor McLean. We are now married for five (5) years and our marriage is has never been stronger.

I never had a desire to be a worship leader or even to write songs. Now the gift in me has been stirred up. I've been writing songs and I'm a praise and worship leader. My husband and I are growing in the anointing. We have changed in everyway you can imagine. I believe this would not have been possible without the right connection with Worship and Faith International Fellowship. Indeed, where the Spirit of the Lord is, there is liberty. We can boldly testify that our lives will never be the same again because we have encountered a new beginning." (Kayson and Viveen Barnaby)

9. Stay Connected

Stay connected by attending church regularly. Don't miss the services for flimsy reasons. Remember, the Lord told us in **Hebrews 10:25 to** *"Not forsake the assembling of ourselves together, as the manner of some is; but exhorting one another: and so much the more, as ye see the day approaching"*

Remember to soak yourself in the messages that flow from the house. This will lead to spiritual growth and deepen the bond between yourself and the man or woman of God you are to honour.

10. Receive Correction with a Graceful Spirit

The bible places special emphasis on submission to spiritual authorities. I cannot emphasize this enough as it is one of the sore points of ministry. The writer says in **Hebrews 13:17** *"Obey those who rule over you, and be submissive, for they watch out for your souls, as those who must give account. Let them do so with joy and not with grief, for that would be unprofitable for you."*

Ministers have a responsibility to circumcise spiritual sons. They must skillfully use the word to cut away flesh **(Genesis 17:10-14).** Always remember, whomever the Lord loves, He corrects. Correction received is a clear sign of honour and respect. Ministers are charged by God to *"Rebuke and to admonish with love"* **(2Timothy 4:2).**

If you've been corrected or rebuked, do not stay away, instead avail yourself to be used in the ministry. Attend church faithfully and show that you're eager to follow your leadership. Look for opportunities to use your gifts and talents for the work of Christ. Do not allow offense or shame to keep you away.

11. *Stand with Your Pastor through Tough Times*

Jesus said, *"You have stood by me in the troubles that have tested me"* (**Luke 22:28**). Every minister will go through testing seasons. Be a REAL friend during those times; a genuine friend who remains steadfast with him regardless of what comes. A genuine friend stands with you during adverse circumstances; does not forsake you when others may abandon you; helps guard you when you are off guard; helps hold you accountable to your values, and forgives and encourages you if or when you fail. Be a friend to your pastor. Do not stay away - send a card or a gift of appreciation that shows your support. Notice that when Jesus was being tested in Gethsemane, He asked his disciples if they could not stand, watch or pray with him for an hour. I encourage you to stand with your pastor.

12. *Stay focused on the Big Picture*

The big picture is JESUS... doing His will. This encompasses loving each other, forgiving one another and seeking to advance and increase the Kingdom of God. Staying focus will help to build God's Kingdom and indeed you will be rewarded.

Remember, if you are faithful over that which belongs to another man, God will give you your own. *"And if ye have not been faithful in that which is another man's, who shall give you that which is your own?"*(**Luke 16:12**).

If you are able to do these 12 things to honour your pastor you are on your way to success! Congratulations.

A General died: The Honour Package

Years ago I witnessed something that changed my life. A great man of God went home to be with the Lord. He had served his church for over 25 years. The church said his elderly widow could not afford the manse (church house). This pastor had given his 'life' to the church, would the church now put out his widow? Where would the honour for the man of God be?

A pastor's daughter once told me that she would never marry a pastor, because she had seen how her dad had sacrificed for the work of the Lord and the church treated him with dishonour. The children of ministers must see the reward and honour that come with the sacrifice and hard work of a pastor so that they too will want to work to advance the kingdom of God from the front. For the scripture says, *"thou shalt not muzzle the ox that treadeth out the corn. And, The labourer is worthy of his reward."* (**1Timothy 5:18.**).

Ministers are hard workers who toil for the kingdom and as such should be rewarded. Those who dedicate their days and night to the Kingdom without being otherwise employed should be compensated so that they can make provisions for their family and future.

If a pastor cannot adequately provide for his family, he will be distracted from the ministry. The sad truth is that many local churches are without adequate "welfare packages" for their leaders. The Psalmist David clearly states in **Psalm 37:25** *"I have been young, and now am old; yet have I not seen the righteous forsaken, nor his seed begging bread."* Ensure that this does not start with your pastor. It is commanded by the Lord as a part of your act of love.

I believe that consideration should be taken to put in place some remuneration package for all fulltime ministers. The church should take care of them. This remuneration package can be altered periodically based on the structure and affordability of the church. The remuneration should be able to cover expenses such as: housing, laundry, travelling, vehicle maintenance, utility, insurance (life & health), vacation, training and development.

My suggestion is that every church should establish a Pastoral Care Committee responsible for caring for the pastor as well as other ministers. After all, your pastor will have similar expenses like any other family. In fact, in some cases, he may have much more due to added expenses such as reading materials necessary for preparing messages, transportation to church events or the way he is expected to represent the ministry.
Pastors should not live in a "hand to mouth" situation, hoping to be blessed with a love gift by a generous brother or sister. A pastor's position is similar to that of a CEO. These persons are normally very well compensated. This promotes loyalty, breeds morale and usually results in them

being more focused. If churches are in a position to take care of their ministers in this way, they should do so with love and joy.

Appreciation Service

An appreciation service should be organized by the pastoral care committee annually by the ministry to which the pastor is attached. Members and friends of the ministry should be invited to participate in a well planned show of appreciation for your spiritual leader.

Every department in the church should seek to get involve. One of the worst things that can happen is for a pastor to literally pour himself out into the lives of those under his care and when his people receive an opportunity to display honour, they do not make the sacrifice. Honouring will generally require you to do three things:

- make *adjustments* to accommodate the one you are honouring,
- make *sacrifices* despite previous plans because the one being honoured is deserving and

- a determination to use every opportunity to give honour.

The Pastors Time

The most important resource for a pastor is his time. Relieve him/her of unnecessary tasks when possible. This will grow the ministry and allow him more time to seek the Lord and prepare himself. This is also a major key in honouring your minister. What are you doing to make the job of your man of God easier? What are you doing to honour your man/woman of God?

5

Honouring All Ministers of the Gospel

"A prophet is honored everywhere except in his own hometown and among his own family" Matthew 13:57

Charity begins at home. It should be the objective of every member of a local church to *want* to honour their ministers. The members are the ones who benefit most from the ministers. It is for you that they constantly seek God so that when you arrive they have a word from God that speaks directly into your situation to the extent that you think they were at home with you and know of your situation personally.

They are the ones who visit you when you or other family members are hospitalized. You are the ones they pray for constantly and they are the ones you seek out when your family is in need of help in any way. Don't they deserve to be honoured by you?

Why not change the present status quo and begin to appreciate those ministers that are right there in your congregation. These include evangelists, prophets, teachers and apostles who visit your church.

Most evangelists, prophets, teachers and apostles are not cared for by the church simply because they are not pastoring the "helm of the ship." The Apostle Paul said in **Philippians 4:15-18** :

> *Now ye Philippians know also, that in the beginning of the gospel, when I departed from Macedonia, no church communicated with me as concerning giving and receiving, but ye only. For even in Thessalonica ye sent once and again unto my necessity. Not because I desire a gift: but I desire fruit that may abound to your account. But I have all, and abound: I am full, having received of Epaphroditus the things which were sent from you, an odour of a sweet smell, a sacrifice acceptable, wellpleasing to God.*

As mentioned earlier, functioning as an evangelist was quite an adventure for me. Many churches would invite me to share God's word. I would go with great zeal with the word of God in my heart and minister with all I had. At the end of the sermon or event, many came with a hearty "Thank-you" and "God bless you". Few considered the cost of full time ministry. I did this for a long while without being compensated. Many told me we can't pay you, God will do it. Repeatedly I was leaving engagements without any consideration for my expenses.

One day, I left a crusade after ministering with absolutely no cash in my wallet and no gas in my car (can you believe it happened again?). I remembered that I drove home quite slowly praying that God would take me home safely without the car shutting down as the gas needle was on empty. I was also quite hungry and there was no food in my house! Might I add that I was now married! Yes, I was and it was my responsibility to take care of my wife. How was I to do that if at the end of each event all I get is a thank you and a God bless you? I hold firm to the belief that full time ministers, who do not have secular jobs, should be compensated for their work in the Kingdom. They do the work of the Lord, therefore our fellow brothers and sister should ensure that they are compensated and not be begging bread.

I am not referring to hirelings, charlatans or soothsayers. I am speaking about people who are genuinely called and sold out for Christ and are given specific responsibilities within their local church. It is important that they are given a stipend to support their financial requirements. Many of them have a family to care for and they must do so adequately. If a minister does not take care of his family, it means that he is going against the word of God. **1Timothy 5:8** says *"But if any provide not for his own, and especially for those of his own house, he hath denied the faith, and is worse than an infidel."* Friends, I am sure that is not the kind of person you want leading you.

I am not saying that the church is obligated to take care of all the needs of a minister – not at all. Paul made tents for a living while ministering, so ministers are encouraged to operate in a similar fashion. If a minister is in a position to use his skills to earn an income, he should do so - whether or not the church is able to take care of his needs. This is not to say that he should be encouraged to focus on the secular task more than his call to ministry (evangelism, apostle, teacher etc) because the minister needs to spend time in the word and seeking God. Some will argue that not all ministers are called into full-time ministry, and I definitely agree. Those who are called must make full proof of their ministry **(2Timothy 4:5).**

If you are in full time church ministry let God lead you! Ask him to speak to you about your role in the church. We should always use wisdom, understanding and seek God's divine will for our lives. Oftentimes churches with ministers with secular jobs are generally limited in the gospel. I am sure you will agree with me that this is a possibility since the minister has to share his time evenly and ethically. He cannot use his employer's time to do work for the church. *"Servants, be obedient to them that are [your] masters according to the flesh, with fear and trembling, in singleness of your heart, as unto Christ;"* *(***Ephesians 6:5)**. Paul's tent making profession was some-what like his own business. That is, he was self-employed. He made tents on his own time until he began to plant churches in different cities. Likewise a minister just starting out in ministry must do whatever he can to sustain himself and his family until the ministry has grown and he is able to dedicate his time fully to it.

Take Care of our Guest Ministers

When an evangelist, prophet, teacher or apostle is invited to a church or event to minister it is standard protocol that the man/woman of God be honoured with a love gift. A love gift should always be prepared prior to their arrival. This should be *monetary*. A card expressing your appreciation can also be attached to the envelope. You should avoid presenting them with personal items unless this was previously discussed and agreed on. The idea of a love gift is two-fold. It is a :

1. *Token of Appreciation* - Something tangible for their contribution and for accepting your invitation and

2. *Remuneration* – This should not be limited to expenses directly relating to the ministry but it should be above.

My suggestion is that ministries have a structured policy in place which will guide them concerning how much should be paid out.

There are many other factors to be considered as we aim to honour visiting ministers and to make them feel welcomed. In doing so, it is important to look at issues such as:

- *Geographical location/proximity:*
  - Are they traveling from another parish/state or country?
  - How long will it take them to get to you?
  - Will they require a pick-up service?

  - Will they require accommodation? A minister went to share God's word and needed accommodation. The local church had one of their members open up his house to the man of God. To his surprise, upon arriving he was greeted at the door with these words: *"Do not wear your shoes in my house!"* Can you imagine? Proper care must be taken in this regard.

- *Hospitality*

  o Are you prepared to administer to their needs?

  o What are their meal (food and beverage) preferences?

  o What are their requirements before and after ministering?

  o Will they need a separate area to prepare themselves before ministering?

  o Will they be accompanied by others?

  o How many seats should be reserved for their travelling associates?

  o Are you expected to cater for the additional guests? (If your budget allows you to cater for additional guests, please do so).

  o Is the hospitality team aware of their expectations?

  o Have you assigned specific team members to deal with the various areas and specific needs of the guests?

The key thing to do here Friends is to be PREPARED. If we are honouring someone, we should not find ourselves scampering about in panic upon their arrival simply because we failed to prepare. Why delay? Let us not be like Naaman the Leper whose pride and lack of faith prevented him from giving honour to Elisha upon his arrival. This story is recorded in **2 Kings 5:14-16:**

*¹⁴Then went he down, and dipped himself
seven times in Jordan, according to the
saying of the man of God: and his flesh
came again like unto the flesh of a little
child, and he was clean. ¹⁵And he returned
to the man of God, he and all his company,
and came, and stood before him: and he
said, Behold, now I know that there is no
God in all the earth, but in Israel: now
therefore, I pray thee, take a blessing of thy
servant. ¹⁶But he said, As the LORD liveth,
before whom I stand, I will receive none.
And he urged him to take it; but he refused.*

Is it that we are waiting to see how "good" this
evangelist will be? Is it that we want to
compensate the prophet based on how many
prophesies are delivered? Will we wait to see how
many persons got delivered? I often warn my
congregation about delayed obedience.

Naaman went to the wrong person in the first place
– the King of Syria and not the Prophet Elisha.
When he eventually got to the "right place",
Naaman was obviously not pleased by the fact that
Elisha did not go out to meet him, a man of such

high esteem among his peers. Elisha instead sent his servant with the message that he should go and dip into the Jordon River. Not once nor twice but in fact seven times. Friends, this sounds like a sermon for next Sunday's service.

Could it be possible that the man of God knew Naaman's heart? *"Now Naaman, captain of the host of the king of Syria, was a great man with his master, and honourable, because by him the LORD had given deliverance unto Syria: he was also a mighty man in valour, but he was a leper."* **(2 Kings 5:1).** Maybe he sensed his pride and lack of faith. Can you imagine how Naaman, this proud and victorious man who was second in command in the Kings army felt?

First, he was led by a slave who served his wife to a strange place, deemed as the enemy's territory, for healing. Second, he was told by a "prophet" (he was very skeptical of Elisha) to go and "bathe" in the very filthy River Jordan! Now that is what we call *"brokenness."* Some may say it was out of desperation but I believe it was God's way of showing Naaman that it pays to be obedient and that he should have prepared for the prophet as the Shunemite woman did in **2Kings 4:8-17:**

> *...and it fell on a day, that Elisha passed to Shunem, where was a great woman; and she constrained him to eat bread. And so it was, that as oft as he passed by, he turned in thither to eat bread. And she said unto her husband, Behold now, I perceive that this is an holy man of God, which passeth by us continually. Let us make a little chamber, I pray thee, on the wall; and let us set for him there a bed, and a table, and a stool, and a candlestick: and it shall be, when he cometh to us that he shall turn in thither. And it fell on a day, that he came thither, and he turned into the chamber, and lay there. And he said to Gehazi his servant, Call this Shunammite. And when he had called her, she stood before him. And he said unto him, Say now unto her, Behold, thou hast been careful for us with all this care; what is to be done for thee? wouldest thou be spoken for to the king, or to the captain of the host? And she answered, I dwell among mine own people. And he said, What then is to be done for her? And Gehazi answered, Verily she*

hath no child, and her husband is old. And he said, Call her. And when he had called her, she stood in the door. And he said, About this season, according to the time of life, thou shalt embrace a son. And she said, Nay, my lord, thou man of God, do not lie unto thine handmaid. And the woman conceived, and bore a son at that season that Elisha had said unto her, according to the time of life.

Let us go back to what happened with Naaman. After Naaman got his healing, he *then* decided to honour Elisha. Sadly for him, Elisha did not take his gift. How many of you believe that when you honour your ministers, you are in deed moving in obedience and by extension also honouring God? Friends, you are and don't be fooled, great is your reward for God himself will honour you in due season, *"..for them that honour me I will honour, and they that despise me shall be lightly esteemed."* **(1 Samuel 2:30).**

Let us not be led by the "Naaman" spirit – let us not think of ourselves better than those who minister to us. Let us not treat our ministers based on their title. The word of the Lord says **"honour all men"**. This includes our evangelists, prophets, apostles and teachers, NOT just your Pastor. In fact, this applies to all members in your church, home, workplace and wherever you may go. **1Peter 2:13-17** said

> *Submit yourselves to every ordinance of man for the Lord's sake: whether it be to the king, as supreme; Or unto governors, as unto them that are sent by him for the punishment of evildoers, and for the praise of them that do well. For so is the will of God, that with well doing ye may put to silence the ignorance of foolish men: As free, and not using your liberty for a cloke of maliciousness, but as the servants of God. Honour all men. Love the brotherhood. Fear God. Honour the king.*

6
Honour through Vigilance: Beware of Wolves

There are three (3) kinds of people who minister. You have the:

- DEVELOPING
- DEVELOPED and the
- DECEIVER

The ***developing minister*** will make mistakes as he grows. Notwithstanding his occasional mistakes, he genuinely loves the flock of God. These mistakes can be reduced through mentorship. The developing minister should not be on his own but should be under the tutelage of a senior minister and should wait until hands have been laid on him and he is released at the appropriate time before going out on his own. Timothy was released by the Apostle Paul. *"..neglect not the gift that is in thee, which was given thee by prophecy, with the laying on of the hands of the presbytery."* **(1Timothy 4:14)**. Apolos was also a developing minister whom Acqilla and Priscilla took and explained more accurately the faith as found in **Acts 18:24 - 26**. If the developing ministering is unwilling to wait and submit he could end up being deceived.

Then you have the **developed minister** who is experienced and seasoned as a result should not make the mistakes of a developing minister. He should walk in great grace.

Then you have **the deceiver**, the wolf or the imposter which is where I'd like to focus. Paul speaks of grievous wolves which would seek to devour the flock in **Acts 20:28-30:**

> *"Take heed therefore unto yourselves, and to all the flock, over the which the Holy Ghost hath made you overseers, to feed the church of God, which he hath purchased with his own blood. For I know this, that after my departing shall grievous wolves enter in among you, not sparing the flock. Also of your own selves shall men arise, speaking perverse things, to draw away disciples after them."*

This is similar to Jesus' statements in **Matthew 7:15-23:**

> *"Beware of false prophets, which come to you in sheep's clothing, but inwardly they are ravening wolves. Ye shall know them by their fruits. Do men gather grapes of thorns, or figs of thistles? Even so every good tree bringeth forth good fruit; but a corrupt tree bringeth forth evil fruit. A good tree cannot bring forth evil fruit, neither can a corrupt tree bring forth good fruit. Every tree that bringeth not forth good fruit is hewn down, and cast into the fire. Wherefore by their fruits ye shall know them. Not every one that saith unto me, Lord, Lord, shall enter into the kingdom of heaven; but he that doeth the will of my Father which is in heaven. Many will say to me in that day, Lord, Lord, have we not prophesied in thy name? and in thy name have cast out devils? and in thy name done many wonderful works? And then will I profess unto them, I never knew you: depart from me, ye that work iniquity."*

Four (4) Signs of a Wolf or a Deceiving Minister

- ### *Controlling and manipulative*

False ministers will use manipulation to gain followers. Once people begin to follow them, they scare the individuals into staying with them. They drive fear into their members, threatening that if they leave they will be cursed. In addition, false ministers will try to control the people's personal lives. False ministers operate in a similar fashion to cult leaders. They will even manipulate their followers to get money out of them.

- ### *Deceptive and shady*

Deception is the act of misleading by false appearance or statement. A *deceiving minister* will seek to intentionally twist God's word for personal gain. In the account of the Prophet Baalam in **Numbers 22** we see where he wanted to curse God's people because King Balak would pay him. He knew one way to get them cursed was to get them to live contrary to the word of God. He tried to accomplish this by getting the people of God to intermarry.

Every Christian has a responsibility to be like the Bereans in **Acts 17:11**:

Now the Bereans were of more noble character than the Thessalonians, for they received the message with great eagerness and examined the Scriptures every day to see if what Paul said was true.

We should not be moved solely by the accuracy of a word of knowledge because Baalam was an accurate prophet yet the Apostle Peter warns us of him, *"..which have forsaken the right way, and are gone astray, following the way of Balaam the son of Bosor, who loved the wages of unrighteousness; But was rebuked for his iniquity: the dumb ass speaking with man's voice forbad the madness of the prophet."* **(2 Peter 2:15 & 16).**

Please note that God looks at three things:
- God looks at the **heart** which is **motive.** *"Woe unto them! for they have gone in the way of Cain, and ran greedily after the error of Balaam for reward, and perished in the gainsaying of Core."* (Jude 1:11). Baalam's motive was greed or money.
- God looks at the *character* which is integrity. He should not be crooked. His yea

should be yea and his nay, nay. He should be of a good report **(1 Tim 1:7)**

- God looks at the *message* which should be *balanced*. Rightly divided **(2 Tim 2:15).**

What will God find when He examines these areas of your life? Would you have followed the wolf or will you remain steadfast and diligent in the word of God.

• *Soothsaying*

The deceptive preacher preaches what people want to hear. Prophesying what people want to hear as oppose to what God is saying. The deceiving minister is a soothsayer (fortune-teller).

• *Gifted yet fruitless*

The gifts of the spirit must not be confused with the fruit of the spirit. A false minister can display a variety of the gifts of the spirit, but cannot fake the fruit of the spirit. This person lacks character. Generally when the gifts are displayed they are not accompanied by manifestation or results. **1 Cor. 12:7-10** states

> *But the manifestation of the Spirit is given to every man to profit withal.[8] For to one is*

given by the Spirit the word of wisdom; to another the word of knowledge by the same Spirit; [9] *To another faith by the same Spirit; to another the gifts of healing by the same Spirit;* [10] *To another the working of miracles; to another prophecy; to another discerning of spirits; to another divers kinds of tongues; to another the interpretation of tongues.*

Galatians 5:22 says *"But the fruit of the Spirit is love, joy, peace, longsuffering, gentleness, goodness, faith."* While **Ephesians 5:9** says *"For the fruit of the Spirit is in all goodness, righteousness, and truth."*

1 Cor. 13:1-6

"Though I speak with the tongues of men and of angels, and have not charity, I am become as sounding brass, or a tinkling cymbal. [2] *And though I have the gift of prophecy, and understand all mysteries, and all knowledge; and though I have all faith, so that I could remove mountains, and have not charity, I am nothing.* [3] *And though I bestow all my goods to feed the poor, and*

though I give my body to be burned, and have not charity, it profiteth me nothing. [4] Charity suffereth long, and is kind; charity envieth not; charity vaunteth not itself, is not puffed up, [5] Doth not behave itself unseemly, seeketh not her own, is not easily provoked, thinketh no evil; [6] Rejoiceth not in iniquity, but rejoiceth in the truth."

The above scriptures clearly detailed what character your man of God should have. If you are a part of a ministry and you do not see these qualities manifested in your ministry I suggest you begin to seek God, asking Him to reveal to you the house to which you are connected and prepare to run!

A true minister is never motivated to enter the ministry because he sees it as a career option. The ministry is not a career option it is a call!! It's not for those who are seeking to make some money or can't find anything else to do. God called Moses, Jeremiah, Paul and Timothy and we behold the fruit of their ministry. If you are a church leader, did God call you? If so make full proof of your ministry and show forth fruit.

7

A Culture of Honour

To have a culture of honour is to have an atmosphere where people are loved, valued and respected. Culture is defined as the set of shared attitudes, values, goals, and practices that characterize an institution, organization or group (SOURCE). As discussed earlier to honour is to value. Anything of value is perceived as being costly, beloved and precious. The way one thinks, will encourage a particular behavior which sometimes lead to habits. Habits create atmosphere and atmosphere creates culture. Strive to create a culture of honour in your house of worship.

Years ago I met a young man who had recently received Jesus as his Lord and saviour. He was a rough guy from the streets. He could hardly read or write. One day, I had a scheduled counseling session. The person was running late. I noticed the young man sitting by himself so I went over to him and asked if he wanted to talk. We sat and spoke for approximately 30 minutes. It was a good talk for both of us. I had no idea of the impact this 30 minutes would have on our lives. This young man saw my action as an act of honour. He felt valued and loved I would take time out to talk with him.

Years after he still remembered and expressed his gratitude for "the little talk" we had and told me how he felt. He informed me that he was doing far better in life and even offered to sow a seed of $100,000 toward a personal project. Friends, I use this as a lesson to all that we should honour everyone. This is a clear indicator that we should not be respecters of persons. We should not deal with persons based on their position or status in life, or our perception of them. We should just love people! **Acts 10:34** *"Then Peter opened his mouth, and said, of a truth I perceive that God is no respecter of persons."*

You never know how things will work out or how the tables may turn in life. I am not saying that you should do acts of kindness with an ulterior motive. I am saying honour all men according to the word of God, in doing so you will be honouring God. The bible says *"be careful to entertain strangers for in so doing many have entertained angels unaware" (Hebrews 13:12).* Allow those who are around you to feel a sense of value and worth. This might not be the easiest thing. People are not always easy to deal with. Most people have been hurt, misused and abused resulting in mistrust. Avoid being one of those people who consistently cause hurt. Sow love instead. Who knows, you may be entertaining angels.

Hindrances to Honour

I'd like to give an illustration of a street dog - a dog that has been abused and rejected. As a result of actions done to him he developed traits that were not originally a part of his character. If you see this wounded dog and decide to help him several things are likely to happen:

- The fear of people may cause the dog to be defensive
- The memory of being abused may cause the dog to attack
- The fear of being rejected again may cause the dog to withdraw and appear anti social.
- The closer you get to the hurting dog to assist him, the more aggressive he may become towards you.

What will you do them? Would your desire to help him fade or will you see the hurt in him and persevere? You will have to make a decision whether you will turn away and leave the dog or cushion yourself to deal with the attacks and win his trust so you are able to minister to him. Similarly, in our quest to honour God we need to persevere and look behind the angry and hurtful words spoken by our brethrens and see wounded hearts in an effort to help them. Remember hurting people hurt others. Are you up to it?

It will be difficult to honour these people without following certain principles:

- **Be quick to forgive and do not take on offense!** *"Then Peter came to Jesus and asked him, "Lord, how often do I have to forgive a believer who wrongs me? Seven times, Jesus answered him, I tell you, not just seven times, but seventy times seven."* (Matthew 18:21-22)
- **Don't keep record of wrongs!** *"Love isn't rude. It doesn't think about itself. It isn't irritable. It doesn't keep track of wrongs."*(1 Corinthians 13:5)

- **Deal with conflicts based on the Word of God.** *"Moreover if thy brother shall trespass against thee, go and tell him his fault between thee and him alone: if he shall hear thee, thou hast gained thy brother. But if he will not hear thee, then take with thee one or two more, that in the mouth of two or three witnesses every word may be established. And if he shall neglect to hear them, tell it unto the church: but if he neglects to hear the church, let him be unto thee as a heathen man and a publican."(* Matthew 18:15-17)

- **Affirm those around you**. We must learn to recognize people's God-given identity and call. While Gideon was acting like a coward and hiding from the enemy, the angel of God called unto Gideon *"The LORD is with thee, thou mighty man of valour. And there came an angel of the LORD, and sat under an oak which was in Ophrah, that pertained unto Joash the Abiezrite: and his son Gideon threshed wheat by the winepress, to hide it from the Midianites. And the angel of the LORD appeared unto him, and said unto him, The*

LORD is with thee, thou mighty man of valour."(**Judges 6:11-12)**

My friends, honour is about giving. It's by no means built around "what I need" it is built around "what I can give" and if I don't learn to give it to those who deserve it least, I will continue to live in an atmosphere without honour.

About a year after giving my heart to Jesus, I backslide. I was still going to church but I went back to my old way of drinking, flirting and cursing. My mother knew it, but she kept saying "Son, you are a man of God. I see you preaching all over the world." She never condemned me! My conscience was doing a pretty good job at that. She merely affirmed my position in Christ.

One day she asked me to pray for her sister. I was skeptical. *What's wrong with mom? Isn't she aware of how I've been living?"* I thought. Nevertheless, as an obedient son I started the prayer with personal repentance and continued on to pray for my aunt. At the end of praying for my aunt I still felt like praying and I continued. The presence of God touched me and I started to repent again. The delivering power of God was released and since that day I've been free! This occurred simply because my mother honoured me, by affirming my identity in Christ. Do you know someone that you need to affirm his/her identify in Christ? If so go ahead today and do it. This may make a big difference in their lives as it did in mine.

In our church we've developed a culture of calling people "man of God" and "woman of God". It's not that everyone is living "right"; sometimes they are living the opposite, just like Gideon, but like the angel, we affirm them. We do not condemn them. By failing to honour those closest to us, we could be cutting off several connections and opportunities of blessing.

In my earlier years, I learnt to dishonour by associating with leaders who dishonoured other leaders. The scripture says in **1Cor. 15:33** *"don't let anyone deceive you. Associating with bad people will ruin decent people. Evil communication corrupts good manners."* In order to become a people of honour, we must be willing to stop the mouths of people who are acting dishonourably through kingdom confrontation.

CONSEQUENCES/ CURSES OF DISHONOURING

- **The spirit of death comes upon such a person.** Matthew 15:4 *"For God commanded, saying, Honour thy father and mother: and, He that curseth father or mother, let him die the death."*
- **Shortened lifespan and it will not be well with thee.** Ephesians 6:2,3 *"thy father and mother; (which is the first commandment with promise;),That it may be well with thee, and thou mayest live long on the earth."*
- **Unfulfilled prophecies.** 1 Samuel 2:30 *"Wherefore the LORD God of Israel saith, I said indeed that thy house, and the house of thy father, should walk before me for ever: but now the LORD saith, Be it far from me; for them that honour me I will honour, and they that despise me shall be lightly esteemed."*

ADVANTAGES/ BLESSINGS IN HONOURING

- **Honour releases life and Favour** (it will be well with thee). Ephesians 6:2,3 *"Honour thy father and mother; which is the first commandment with promise;That it may be well with thee, and thou mayest live long on the earth."*

- **Stirs the supernatural.** Ruth honoured Naomi. As a result, supernatural connection, blessings and favour were released. Read Ruth Chapters 1-3.

Let's invade this evil culture of dishonouring with God's love! I guarantee you that as you build a culture of honour in your home, work and church unprecedented breakthroughs will manifest in your life.

Friends, I honour You!!

PRAYER

L ord, I honour you as my King and Saviour.
There is no one like you. I praise and worship
Your holy name. Lord, I repent for the times when
I fail to give You the honour that You deserve. I
also repent for times when I may not have
honoured the leadership that You have set over
me.

I thank You for the power of Your word and today
I choose to honour Your word above my opinion
and that of others. Take first place in my life today
O Sovereign Lord, in Jesus' name.

Please grant me the grace to live a life that honours
You. Help me to honour the people I come in
contact with daily, even when it's difficult. Grant
me the grace to honour You on the job, at home
and at church.

Lord, please grant me the grace to honour You
with my substance and my increase.

I declare that I am submissive! I am not a rebel!
Lord, I receive Your forgiveness and Your love.

I thank You that I am not condemned but forgiven.

Lord, Your word declares that if I confess my sins You are faithful and just to forgive me of my sins and cleanse me of all unrighteousness. Therefore, I declare that I am the righteousness of God in Christ Jesus.

I now receive the manifestation of Your blessing!

The favour and peace of God is all over me, in Jesus' name! Amen!! Amen!! Amen!!

Made in the USA
Middletown, DE
03 September 2024

60246848R00076